Meet the Lithographer
Written and illustrated by Gaby Bazin

Published by
David Zwirner Books
520 West 20th Street, 3rd Floor
New York, New York 10011
+ 1 212 727 2070
davidzwirnerbooks.com

Editors: Doro Globus and Jessica Palinski
Proofreaders: Chris Peterson and Chandra Wohleber
Translator: Vineet Lal

Printer: TNM Print

Typeface: Nanami Rounded Pro
Paper: Munken Print Cream 150 gsm

Publication © 2023 David Zwirner Books
Text and illustrations © 2021 Éditions MeMo
Translation © 2023 Vineet Lal

First published in 2021 in French by Éditions MeMo

ISBN: 978-1-64423-110-4
Library of Congress Control Number: 2023901462

Printed in the Czech Republic

MEET THE LITHOGRAPHER

Written and illustrated by **Gaby Bazin**

Translated by Vineet Lal

David Zwirner Books

Welcome to my lithography studio!

This is where I use a special technique to create pictures. It's almost like magic.

First, I draw on a flat piece of stone. Then I copy my artwork, thanks to this imposing machine called a press.

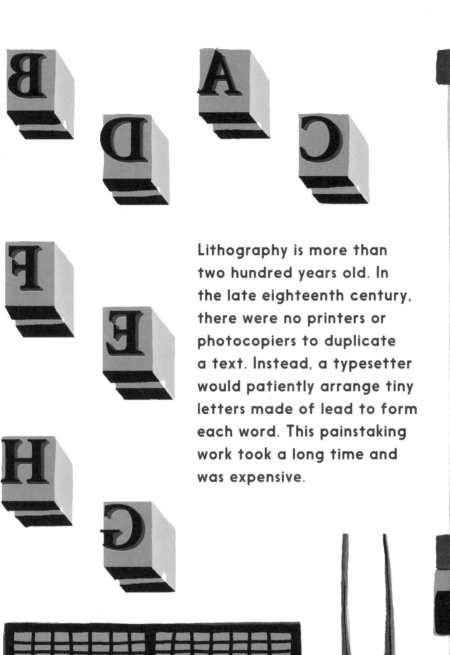

Lithography is more than two hundred years old. In the late eighteenth century, there were no printers or photocopiers to duplicate a text. Instead, a typesetter would patiently arrange tiny letters made of lead to form each word. This painstaking work took a long time and was expensive.

Around the same time, in Germany, a young man with a passion for the theater, Alois Senefelder, was desperately seeking a publisher for his plays. Having failed many times, he decided to print his work himself. But his father had just died and Alois had to take care of his eight brothers and sisters. He didn't have a penny to his name, and he had no way of buying the tools and equipment he needed.

So Alois began to experiment.
He was relentless.

He imprinted the shapes
of letters into wax.

He engraved metal plates.

He chiseled into stones
found in a riverbed,
using a sharp tool
called a burin.

Nothing could stop him.
But nothing worked.

One day, his mother said to him,
"Alois, the cleaner is here for the laundry.
Quick, jot this down: one coat, three shirts,
two pairs of long johns . . ."

Because he couldn't find any paper,
Alois wrote the list on a stone slab.
That's when he had an idea. He poured
some acid on the stone, hoping it would
etch away the surface around the
writing. Next, Alois spread some
ink on the stone, laid a sheet
of paper on top, rubbed the
paper . . . and ended up
with a copy of the list.

Overjoyed, he carried on with his research. He concocted recipes for ink, discovered a thousand ways of preparing his stones, and turned himself into an amateur chemist. Finally, by the late 1790s, the process was working smoothly. Alois Senefelder became the official inventor of lithography—the first method of printing from a flat surface.

You must be wondering
how we do this today.
Let me show you!

First, I choose a beautiful piece of stone. A slab of limestone, nice and heavy, will soak up oil and water like a sponge.

A single stone can be used to print hundreds of different pictures. But before I start drawing, I need to erase the previous image completely.

I sprinkle the slab with sand and add a little water.

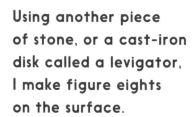

Using another piece of stone, or a cast-iron disk called a levigator, I make figure eights on the surface.

I carry on working without feeling tired, soothed by the grinding of the sand. One last rinse and the picture has vanished! Lithography is my favorite sport.

The stone is blank,
ready to store a future image
in its memory.

A lithography stone loves anything greasy.
You could even draw on it with oil or potato chips!

But I prefer using:

litho pencils

feathers

thin brushes

wide brushes

chalk

or mechanical pencils.

A lithographic artist can also:

make wash drawings with ink

scrape with a pointy instrument

rub with chalk

spatter ink with a toothbrush

make finger marks

or scribble with a litho pencil.

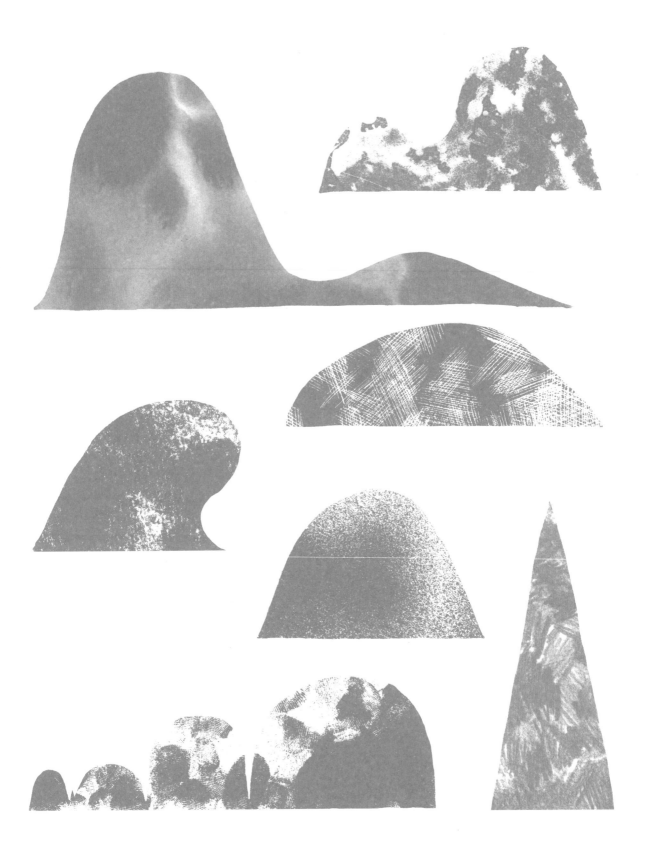

When the picture is finished, it needs to be set into the stone. I smear it with a sticky mixture of water, gum arabic, and nitric acid.

Then I let it rest overnight. The drawing sinks into the stone, which absorbs it and saves it in its memory.

Now I can wipe away the image by rubbing it with turpentine.

It has disappeared, but it will reappear shortly. Soon we'll be able to print it at last.

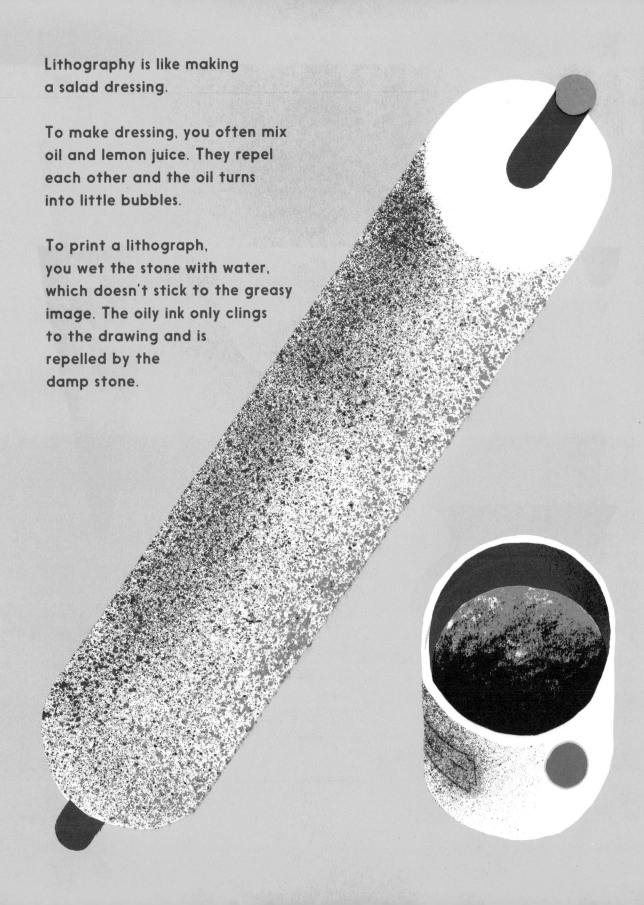

Lithography is like making
a salad dressing.

To make dressing, you often mix
oil and lemon juice. They repel
each other and the oil turns
into little bubbles.

To print a lithograph,
you wet the stone with water,
which doesn't stick to the greasy
image. The oily ink only clings
to the drawing and is
repelled by the
damp stone.

Lithographic ink
has a texture like
chewing gum. It needs
to be spread evenly
with a big roller.

I wet the stone with a sponge,
run the ink roller across it,
and the magic begins.

The color reveals
the drawing.

Now I place a sheet of paper on top, and our stone passes under the press. This enormous machine has a nickname: the horned beast.

When I turn the wheel, the press pushes the paper against the stone with tremendous force. For a print the size of this book, it would be as if ten elephants were sitting on it!

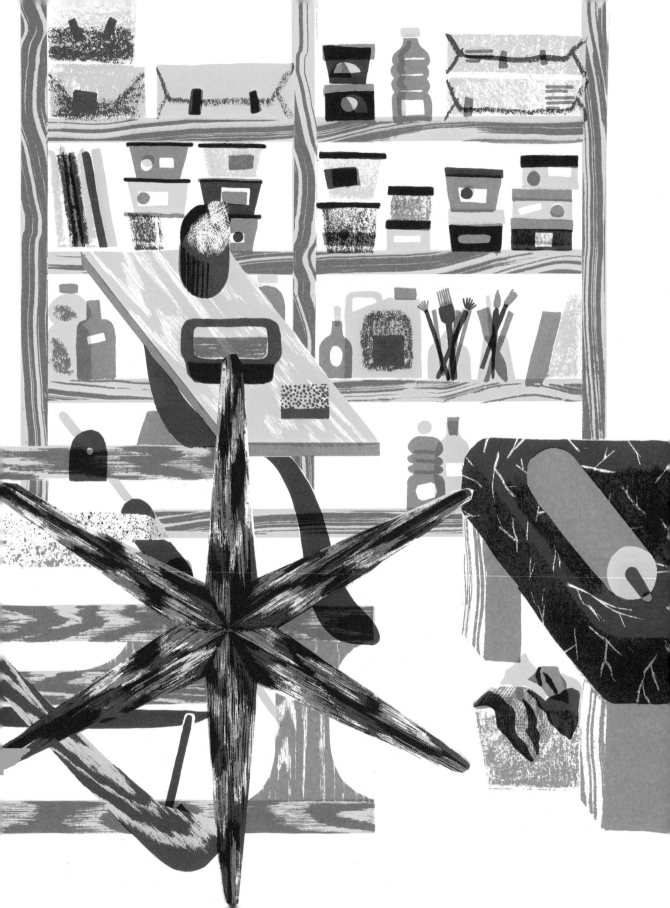

Whatever you print is reversed on the paper, as if seen in a mirror. So I imagine my pictures and words the other way around as I draw on my stone.

In lithography,
colors can be layered
on top of one another.

With just three stones
inked with

blue

red

yellow

you can make a
whole rainbow.

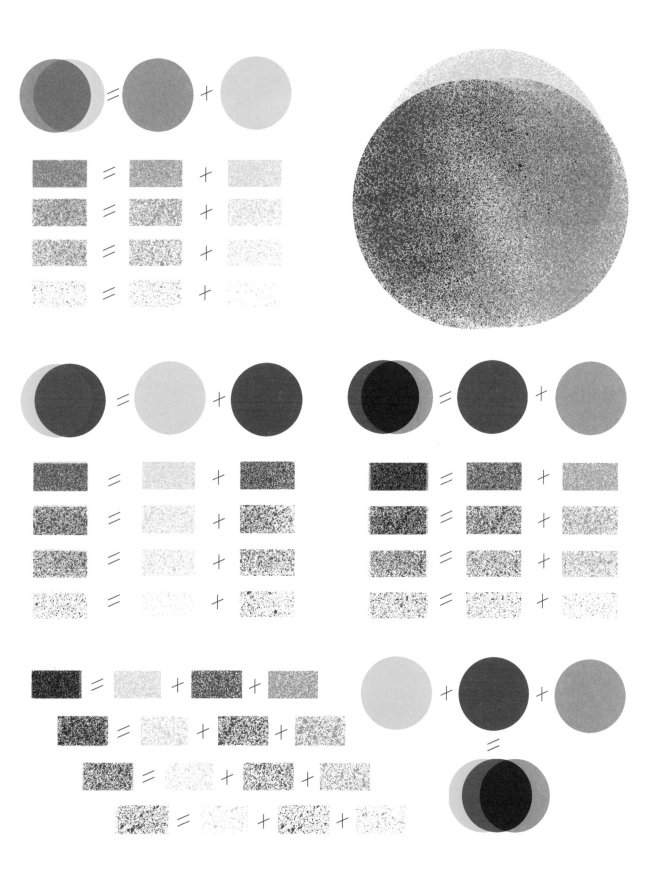

Lithography became wildly successful soon after its invention. Thanks to this technique, it was possible to print music scores and caricatures, to make colored copies of paintings, to produce huge posters, and to publish books for children.

Today books are no
longer printed using
lithography. But all
over the world, artists
and printmakers like
me continue to work
patiently on their stones
to create precious works
of art.

Lithography has captured the heart of many artists, including the cartoonist and "father of the comic strip" Rodolphe Töpffer

the caricaturist Honoré Daumier

the poster artist Jules Chéret

the author and illustrator Jean Bruller, who wrote as Vercors

the illustrator Nathalie Parain

and artists like Sonia Delaunay, Alexander Calder, and Kiki Smith.

Alois Senefelder never made a fortune from lithography. But his invention certainly made its mark.

It eventually led to offset
lithographic printing—the
process used to print this
book, as well as the magazines,
newspapers, and posters you
see all around you today.